GW00771471

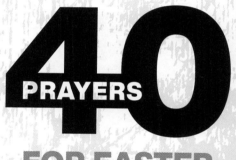

40
PRAYERS
FOR EASTER

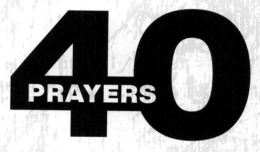

40

PRAYERS

FOR EASTER

**Prayers for your
Church or small group**

DAVID CLOWES

DAVID **C** COOK™

transforming lives together

40 PRAYERS FOR EASTER
Published by David C Cook
4050 Lee Vance Drive
Colorado Springs, CO 80918 U.S.A.

Integrity Music Limited, a Division of David C Cook
Brighton, East Sussex BN1 2RE, England

ISBN 978-0-8307-8235-2
eISBN 978-0-8307-8243-7

© 2021 David Clowes

The Team: Ian Matthews, Jack Campbell,
Jo Stockdale, Susan Murdock
Cover Design: Pete Barnsley

Printed in the United Kingdom
First Edition 2021

1 2 3 4 5 6 7 8 9 10

120120

CONTENTS

INTRODUCTION

Having published *500 Prayers for All Occasions* and *500 More Prayers for All Occasions* I was asked to develop a new series of books of prayer for use in small groups or in the home.

There are at least forty prayers in each of these books based around a single theme. Most of the content comes from my first two books of prayer for public worship, but has been revised and re-worked to make it appropriate for use in churches, small groups, the family situation, or for personal quiet time devotions.

My church background was firmly in the camp of extemporary prayer. I started to write my prayers down due to nervousness and on the advice of my preaching mentor who insisted on careful preparation not only of the hymns, readings, and sermon, but also of the prayers. I have long since realised the value of having a resource to be used as a flexible launch pad for my own prayer life which I could use and adapt as I wished.

I hope that is how you will approach these simple aids to prayer. They have been deliberately written in an uncomplicated style and with language that seeks to illuminate the joy of prayer. I have also tried to ensure that they are written in the language we use in our daily conversations. The aim of this is designed to make them easier to 'pray' and not simply to 'read'.

David Clowes
Stockport, April 2020

PRAYERS OF APPROACH

WE COME

Lord, we come with all our doubts and fears
to be touched with the truth of your resurrection.
We come with all our sorrows and pain
to be held with the hope of your resurrection.
We come with our disappointments and failures
to be strengthened by your resurrection.
We come as we are.
We come for we must.
We come to celebrate your resurrection. **Amen.**

WE COME BECAUSE WE MUST

Lord, we come from a world full of so many things
that tempt us and lead us away from you;
from a world full of despair and anguish and pain.
We come with our concerns and doubts and fears.
We come hurting, tired with the struggle
      and strain of just living.
We come feeling lost and uncertain and just as we are.
We come because you called us.
We come because we must.

We come to give you worship and honour and praise.
We come to make confession and to be made whole.
We come because you came and go on coming,
　　our living Saviour and Lord. **Amen.**

YOU HAVE MADE US

Lord, we come because you have made us.
We come because in Christ we have been made new.
We come because you have given us life.
We come because through the risen Christ
　　we have received new life.
We come as your sons and daughters.
We come to be filled with the Spirit.
We come to hear your promise of eternal life.
We come to worship and be sent out for your glory.
　　Amen.

BECAUSE YOU ARE WORTHY

Lord, we have come to praise you because you are worthy.
We have come to give you thanks
　　because you renew our hope.
We have come to worship you because you walk with us
everywhere and every day of our lives. **Amen.**

IN THE RUSH OF LIFE

Lord, we come because we have heard you calling.
We have heard you in the noise and the rush of life.
We have heard you in the responsibility
　　of home and work.
We have heard you in our times of strength and in our
　　moments of weakness.

We have heard you in our doubts and uncertainties.
We have heard you and known we are unworthy, but still
    we have come.
We have come because you have called
    and we are accepted.
We have come to praise you for your call. **Amen.**

PRAYERS OF PRAISE

THE REASON FOR OUR PRAISES

Wonderful God!
We praise you for the hope and joy of this day
and for the assurance that Christ's resurrection gives us,
that your victory will always have the final word over all
the hurt and sorrow and the darkness of life.
We praise you that we went to the empty cross and we
found a Saviour,
but we praise you more that when we went to the empty
tomb we returned with a Lord.

Wonderful, wonderful God!
We simply cannot find the words that will do justice to
the joy we feel
and to the worship we long to offer you.
We praise you for sharing our sin and our shame,
but we praise you more for the life-renewing light with
which you have flooded our lives.
We praise you for the hope and joy that flowed over those
first witnesses of your rising,
but we praise you more that the same hope and joy that
was theirs
still flows into our hearts and lives today.

We praise you for the way your resurrection rekindles our
     faltering faith,
gives light which breaks into our darkness,
and touches us with the assurance that nothing will ever
     be the same again.
Lord, keep our praises ringing out through the whole of
     your world
that all people everywhere and for ever may join in the
     endless song to your glory. **Amen.**

YOUR PROMISE

Father, we praise you for every opportunity we are given
     to meet together
for worship, fellowship, and praise
and for your promise that whenever we meet
     in the name of Christ
you will be in the midst of us and that your almighty
     presence will make us whole.

We praise you for the way you came to the disciples
when they most needed your presence and when they
     least expected it:
when they had locked themselves in behind the closed
     door of the upper room
you came and gave them your peace;
when they walked on the road to Emmaus
you came and gave them burning hearts
     in place of their despair;
when they returned to their fishing, uncertain of what the
     future held,
you came and shared their meal.

Father, we praise you for your promise to be with us
     always, even to the end and beyond.
We praise you for those times when we have been
     lost and alone,
when we have been uncertain and afraid,
when we have felt imprisoned and filled with despair and
     you have come to us.
You have come when we most needed your presence and
     when we least expected it.
You have come and given us new hope, peace, and joy.
You have not promised that you will always
     remove every problem
or take away every pain.
But you have promised to be with us and to share our
     journey
of life and faith, and for this we praise you.
We praise you for the new life that Christ
     has made possible
and for his coming to live in our hearts and lives.
We ask that you will so fill us with the Holy Spirit
that our worship may be worthy of you, filled with power,
     and may bring you glory. **Amen.**

SHEER JOY

Lord, we praise you that you have not only created all
     things
but also you made each one of us.
We praise you for the life you have given us
and for the sheer joy of being alive to enjoy your world.
We praise you more that you have made us for fellowship
     with you
and with one another that we might experience
     something of the joy and glory

we shall know when we enter the heaven of your love.
We praise you for all that you have done for us in Christ
and for his life lived to the full in your love.
We praise you for his death for us in our place
    as a sign of your grace
and we praise you for his mighty resurrection
and the evidence of your power at work in him.
We praise you that his resurrection power is available
to all who put their trust in him.
We praise you for the power of your Holy Spirit
who fills the whole universe and transforms our lives and
    the life of your church.
You are truly an amazing God!
We praise you that despite our weakness,
our failure, and the frailty of our faith
you still offer us the hope, joy, and power that make all
    things new.
We pray, fill us with your grace
    that we may praise you here
and through the coming days of this week. **Amen.**

UNLIMITED GOD

Living, loving God!
We praise you that your purposes for us are not limited by
    time and space
and your love for us is not bounded by
    our selfishness and sin.
Your grace reaches out for us even when we deliberately
    go our own way
and your truth gives us hope even in the darkest times.
We praise you for Christ,
for his coming to share all that life means to us.

We praise you for his coming in fulfilment
of all your promises
and for his death which has opened the way for us to
know you
and to experience your presence in a whole new way.
Living, loving God!
We praise you for Jesus' amazing resurrection, which fills
us with confidence
and assures us that you have accepted his sacrifice
not only for the sin of the world, but also for our sin and
selfishness too.
We praise you for Christ's coming and walking with us,
for his sharing of our journey.
We ask that you will so fill us with your Holy Spirit
that we might live for your glory and our words and deeds
may honour your name. **Amen.**

THERE IS NO GOD LIKE YOU

Almighty God, our heavenly Father,
we have come to praise you for who you are.
We praise you for your majesty, your authority, your
sovereignty and power.
There is no God like you.
There is no God besides you.
We praise you, the one, true, living Lord of all creation.
You are Lord of all that you have made.
You have authority over all that was, is, and will be.
Yours is the power, yours is the glory, and yours is the
name above all names.
Father, we have come to praise you
for what you have done.
You have made us and loved us.
You have held us and healed us.

You have forgiven us and accepted us.
You have made us your sons and daughters.
You have given us your Son whom we know
both as Jesus our Saviour and Christ our Lord.
We praise you for the living Christ, the Shepherd who
knows all his sheep.
We praise you for his love for those already in the fold
and those who are still far away and have not yet
heard his voice.
We praise you for your Spirit who reaches out,
touches and changes lives, and welcomes us home.
We praise you, our Father and our Shepherd,
for who you are and what you have done
to make us your own.
In the name of the Good Shepherd. **Amen.**

PRAYERS OF THANKSGIVING

JUST THE BEGINNING

Father, we thank you for the certainty that you gave to
    your disciples,
those who had followed you and trusted you and had
    watched you die.
They thought everything they had longed for was all over,
but on Easter Day they discovered
    it was all just beginning.
We thank you for being the God who changes finale
    into overture;
you transform conclusions into introductions
and you turn our ends into your new beginnings.
We thank you for those who have not only followed you
    to the ends of the earth
but to the end of their lives.
We thank you for those who have risked all
because of the promise that we shall share
    in your glorious resurrection.
We thank you for demonstrating that there is nothing,
not even our weakness, our sinfulness, our doubts,
    or our death,

that is stronger than your resurrection power.
We thank you for the promise that no longer will we need
to hang on to the life of faith by the skin of our teeth.
You have promised to fill our lives with the power
that raised Christ from the dead
that we may live victorious lives for Christ.
We thank you that Christ was not only raised
but is raised and is now and always our living Lord.
    Amen.

THE LIFE OF YOUR WORLD

Almighty God, our heavenly Father, we thank you for the
    life of your world
and for the life you have given us.
We thank you for the beauty and wonder of all your creation
and that we have a chance to discover and enjoy it.
We thank you for the varied colours and shapes
    all around us
and for eyes to see it,
for ears to appreciate the sounds of life, and for hearts that
    can simply be thankful.
We thank you for all that you have done for us in your
    Son, Jesus Christ our Lord;
for his life and his ministry on earth;
for his teaching about your kingdom;
and for his parables that made your love real.
We thank you that he died to be our Saviour
and for his rising again as our Lord.
We thank you that we do not worship a dead hero who
    lived long ago
but that our risen and living Lord is with us in all the
    twists and turns of life.

Father, it is because of Christ that we have come.
It is because of what he has done that we can come into
    your almighty presence.
He has opened the way into life that is real and into
    knowing you as our Father.
We thank you for all those whom you have given us
to share our journey of life and of faith together.
We thank you for family and friends
and for those with whom we will share your presence for
    all eternity.
Father, enable us not only to thank you but, by your
    grace, to live thankful lives.
Through Christ our living Lord. **Amen.**

GIFT OF LIFE

Father, we thank you not only for giving us life
but also for giving us new life and hope.
Thank you that the story of Easter is not simply a record
    of something
that happened once, long ago,
but that the power that raised Christ from the dead
is available to us here and now.
We thank you for your assurance that no matter
    who we are
your grace is sufficient for our need;
no matter who we are or what we have done
    or failed to do
your love and power can lift us, hold us,
and transform us into the people you meant us to be from
    the very beginning.
Father, we thank you for all those who, down the
    centuries and all across the world,
have been made new by your love.

We thank you for the way you continue to touch and
    change our lives today
and we thank you more for the way you nourish our lives
with your word of grace and the power of the Holy Spirit.
Lord, we thank you for the knowledge that,
though there are times when we feel empty, you have
    promised to fill us.
Though there are moments when we still feel
    lost and uncertain,
your love continues to reach out and always will.
Though our faith is weak, our witness ineffective,
our service self-centred, and our worship unworthy,
you have the power to make us able to do all things in
    Christ who calls us.
We thank you for every opportunity
    to honour your name
and to be nourished by the presence of the living Christ,
    the true bread of life. **Amen.**

DEPTH OF YOUR LOVE

Father, we thank you for the width of your love that
    reaches out
and goes on reaching to hold us, to touch us, and to draw
    us closer to yourself.
Thank you for the depth of your love
and for the reminder that no matter how deep our
    troubles, problems, or worries
and no matter the anguish we feel or the depth
    of our despair,
your love in Christ still reaches deeper.
You lift us and set us more firmly on the rock of faith.
We thank you that your love is higher and more
    demanding than we can ever imagine.

We thank you that you never let us off, never let us go,
and never let us down.
You never allow us to be satisfied with half-hearted
commitment and second-best obedience.
We thank you that your love is richer than anything we
have known as love before.
You seek to transform our lives by your grace and to
journey with us.
Again and again you surprise us in those moments when
we know we have met with you.
Father, thank you for those whose words and example
brought us the challenge to begin our journey
of faith in you.
Thank you for those who have made your presence known
and your love real.
Thank you for those who have enriched our journey
and set our hearts on fire for you.
May we demonstrate our thankfulness in our
commitment
to share the journey of our neighbours that they may also
journey with you. **Amen.**

THE GOOD SHEPHERD

Father, we thank you for your love for all your creation
and for your love ever-reaching out to a lost and fallen
world.
We thank you for your love unending
and for your love made human in Jesus
who is your love incarnate—
calling, searching, holding, risking everything
in dying and rising.
We thank you for Christ, the Good Shepherd,
who demonstrates the reality and power of your love.

We thank you for all that you accomplished in his life,
    death, and resurrection
and that he is the door to hope and fulfilment, to peace
    and to joy.
We thank you that in him there is
freedom from fear and freedom to live,
freedom to love and freedom to give,
freedom to come and freedom to go,
freedom to thank and freedom to trust,
freedom to love and freedom to care,
freedom to stand firm and freedom for all.
We thank you for those whose lives and words and deeds
have made the love of Christ real for us;
for those who have stood by us, those who have
    tried to understand,
and for those who have loved us no matter the cost.
Father, our Father, we thank you
and ask that we may be shepherds in your name. **Amen.**

PRAYERS OF CONFESSION

CONFESSION OF FAITH

Lord, we make our confession of faith
as we affirm our belief in all you have done for us
in the life, death, and resurrection of Christ.
We confess that too often our confession of faith is simply
     a matter of words
and that, for us, it is empty of any real meaning or impact
     on our lives.
We rejoice that Christ is risen but we are still
     overwhelmed
by the confusion of life and the fear of death.
We say we believe but our selfish lives, our petty
     disagreements,
and our failure to love one another and our neighbours
make a nonsense of our faith in the empty tomb
as it crucifies Christ all over again.
Forgive, cleanse, and renew us.
By the power of your mighty resurrection,
     lift us, restore us,
and make us the people you always meant us to be.
In the name of the risen Christ. **Amen.**

YOU DESIGNED US

Lord, you have made us for fellowship with you and with
   one another.
You have designed our lives to be such that we need you
and without you we can never know a lasting sense of
   peace and purpose.
We confess our foolish attempts to live our lives in our
   own strength and on our own.
We confess that we have again and again turned our backs
   on you
and your love and on the care and the compassion of
   others.
We confess the poverty of our faith and our struggle in
   believing.
We confess that we live as though Christ were still dead
   and not our living Lord.
We confess that we find it easier to trust ourselves than his
   love and power.
Lord, when we are down and filled with despair,
through our own foolishness and pride,
take hold of our hands, put your arm around our
   shoulders, and lead us back to you.
Cleanse and renew our lives that we may live for your
   praise and trust your love. **Amen.**

WE FILL OUR LIVES

Lord, we confess that we seek to fill our lives
with so many things and different experiences.
We spend our time striving for material possessions and
   qualifications
but our lives still lack meaning.
We give greatest honour to family and friends

but still we feel lost and are often quite lonely.
We count as important status and health, our wealth, and
    love of security.
We fill our days with endless activity
but still we are hungry and thirsty and empty.
Lord, we confess our sadness over the way we have
    misused our time, our gifts, and your mercy.
Forgive our self-pity, our criticisms of others, and our love
    of complaining.
By the power of the risen Christ, fill us with your hope
    and your cleansing
and feed us with Christ, the bread of life. **Amen.**

YOU SPEAK

Lord, you speak, but we are deaf.
You call, but we do not want to listen.
You challenge us, but we close our ears.
You hold out your hand to guide and to lift us, but we
    turn away from you.
You reach out to give us your comfort, but we are too self-
    confident to receive it.
You join us on our journey, but we do not recognise you.
You try to change the direction of our lives, but we think
    we know best.
You warm our cold hearts, you inspire our faith,
and you forgive us again and again, and we are amazed.
Lord, open our hearts to your grace
and renew our hope and our faith in Christ our Lord.
    Amen.

WHEN WE FALL

Father, forgive us when we fall,

when we lose our way, or lead others astray because we do
    not listen to your voice.
Forgive us the hurt we cause you and one another
by our angry words and our selfish attitudes.
Forgive us for those we allow to be hungry
    but we do not feed them;
those who are lost but we do not search;
those whose lives are naked and vulnerable
    but we do not care;
those who are imprisoned in fear and loneliness but we
    are not there;
those who are thirsty for love and acceptance
    and life that is real
but we send them away empty-handed.
We confess that there are those who are strangers,
who are different from us but we offer no welcome;
those whose lives are sick and broken and hurting
but we do not offer the name of the Good Shepherd to
    heal them and hold them.
Forgive us, empower us, and send us out in your name.
    Amen.

PRAYERS FOR ALL-AGE WORSHIP

HE'S ALIVE

Lord, we praise you on this day, the day of resurrection,
the day that Jesus Christ has been raised to life again!
Father, you are the source of all that is good and true.
All our hope and joy comes from you.
We come to you on this Easter Day to rejoice with you
    that Jesus Christ is alive!
This is indeed a day of celebration and thanksgiving.
We have discovered in the emptiness of the tomb
that nothing but nothing but nothing
    can ever stop your love
and your utter determination to make our lives new.
We are filled with great joy because Jesus,
who died on the cross that we might be free
and that we might know what it means to call you
    our Father,
is alive and is with us for ever.
We thank you that he shared in the hurt and pain and
    sorrow of our world, and
because of his resurrection he is now the source of hope,
    comfort, and forgiveness for everyone.
Father, we praise you for Easter.

May the joy of this day mean that whatever we face in the
days and years to come,
we may always do so in the knowledge that you are alive
and you are with us.
Give us the assurance that all the things in our lives that
trouble us,
even death itself, have been defeated
and when we put our trust in Jesus we can share in his
wonderful victory.
Forgive us, Father, that we live and speak and act
as though Jesus is still in the tomb or just a good man that
died a long, long time ago.
We pray, forgive us our sin and selfishness,
take away our doubts, answer our questions,
and set us free to know and praise you for ever. **Amen.**

BEING DISCIPLES

Lord, we praise you for your goodness, power, and glory
and we thank you for being so patient with us
in our weakness and understanding, our doubts and fears.
Sometimes we begin to think that we are not worthy to
be your disciples
or that we will be of little or no use to you
in your kingdom.
We read in the Bible about the disciples of Jesus
and we thank you that they were such ordinary people
who, until Jesus called them to follow him, were living
such very ordinary lives,
but they discovered that following him made their lives
extra-ordinary.
We praise you that the Bible tells us of the disciples'
strengths and their weaknesses,
their faith and also their doubts.

We thank you for the questions they asked Jesus
and for the gentle way he responded to their concerns.
We thank you for the story of the call of Matthew
who seemed more interested in money than in you;
for James and John who argued with everybody;
and for Peter who even denied he knew Jesus;
for Thomas who, despite all his doubts and his fears,
found he could put his faith in Jesus
and that the one he had known as his leader
he now knew as Saviour and Lord.
We thank you for those who have helped us to know you
and to put our trust in you.
We ask your forgiveness for those times
when what we say or do and how we behave
make it harder for others to put their trust in Jesus.
Forgive us our bad moods and our cheating
and our always wanting our own way;
forgive us for not really listening to you
and for trying to rely on our own strength;
forgive us and help us to bring joy to others and glory to
    Jesus. **Amen.**

GIFT OF LIFE

Heavenly Father, we praise you for giving us life
and for filling our lives with so many wonderful things;
for giving us health and strength
    and for family and friends
and for the joy of being alive and enjoying
all the different colours and shapes we see all around us;
and we thank you not only that they are there but also
    that we can enjoy them.
We thank you for the different sounds that we can hear.

Everything, from the harmony of a symphony orchestra
    to the beat and rhythm of a rock band,
from the song of a bird to the cry of a baby,
is part of the rich echo of life that touches, changes, and
    moves us.
We thank you that Jesus taught us to ask you for 'our
    daily bread'
and that he knew that you long to give us
    everything we need.
You know we are hungry people.
We are hungry for hope and for joy,
    for peace and for pleasure,
for success and for achievement, for health and for
    strength.
We thank you that whilst you know the things we want
you always give us what we need!
We praise you for bread for our bodies and for the food
    for our minds.
We thank you for feeding our hearts on your word
    in the Bible
and for the deep sense of satisfaction which fills our lives
    when we know Jesus.
Forgive us for trying to find hope, peace, and joy
    anywhere else but in Jesus;
forgive us when we see others hungry for food,
for life, and for love and we do nothing to help them.
Lord, change our minds, change the things
    we think are important,
and change us into the people you always meant us to be.
In the name of Jesus, who feeds us with your grace.
    Amen.

OUR JOURNEY

Father, we praise you for the wonderful gift of life
and that you share every moment of every day of it
        with us;
for filling our journey with so many good things;
and we thank you for things to learn and things to
        discover,
for things to enjoy and for things that give us excitement.
We thank you for friends who share with us and
        play with us
and for our families who help us and love us even when
        we are not very kind to them.
We praise you for Jesus, whose teaching about you and
        your kingdom
makes the journey of life very special
and for his love for us that makes it worthwhile.
We thank you for the story of how Jesus walked on the
        Emmaus Road with two disciples
and how he shared in their disappointment and sadness.
We thank you that he helped them to find hope and a
        new beginning
as he shared his love and himself with them
and for those who have helped us when we were
        sad and afraid;
for those who have guided us even when we did not want
        any help
and for those who have given us hope and listened
to our questions and our doubts and our fears.
We thank you for those who helped us to see Jesus
and for those who made his love and his presence real.
Forgive us that so often we do not want to listen to you
or to others who try to help us when we are down.
Forgive us for not listening to others when we knew they
        were alone.

Forgive us for not forgiving others in the way you
    forgive us.
We ask this in Jesus' name. **Amen.**

LIKE A SHEPHERD

Heavenly Father, we praise you not only for making us
but also for caring for us and helping us.
Though we cannot see you we know that you are always
    with us,
for you have promised to be with us no matter what we
    do or where we go.
We praise you that we can see the signs
    of your being with us
every time we open our eyes and look at the world you
    have made.
We thank you that we know you and your love for us in
    Jesus.
In him you shared in everything that life means to us.
We thank you that he told his disciples that
    he was like a shepherd
and like a shepherd he knows each one of us by name
and he cares about each of us every day;
that like a shepherd he gives us
the things we need for us to grow up strong and healthy
    for him.
We thank you that like a shepherd he wants us
    to know him
as the one who will help us, guide us, lead us,
    and keep us safe.
We thank you for all those who care for us and for those
    who care about us.
We thank you for those who care for us when we are sick
    or in hospital

and we thank you for family and friends
whose love and kindness make each day special.
We thank you that you give us opportunities
        to help other people
and to show them your love and care.
We thank you for the joy we have in making
        other people happy
and for giving them love.
Forgive us when we keep your love and care for ourselves
and when we do not help others when we could.
Forgive us for always wanting the biggest
        and the best of everything
and for being greedy, selfish, and jealous.
Forgive us when we do not want to forgive someone else
and, by your Holy Spirit, give us the strength we need to
        follow Jesus.
We ask this in his name. **Amen.**

PRAYERS OF INTERCESSION

THE GOOD NEWS

We pray for those for whom the good news of Easter is
    just too good to be true;
for those who long to believe but are looking for proof
when none can be given except to the eye of faith;
for those who will only accept what can be
seen, touched, or scientifically confirmed;
for those who dare not believe because of the challenge
to their whole way of thinking and the changes
it would require them to make to their
    whole way of living.
May the risen Christ touch their hearts with his grace.
We ask our prayer,
in the name of Christ.

We pray for those who feel they can go no further;
for those who have lost confidence and courage;
those for whom hope is gone and joy has withered away;
those for whom life no longer holds any promise
and each day is a burden too much to bear;
for those who are ill and those who are dying,
those who care for them and those who ignore them;

for those whose lives are empty
and with the passing years have lost meaning;
for the lonely, alone, and the confused.
May the risen Christ give them his peace.
We ask our prayer,
in the name of Christ.

We pray for the church and all Christians;
for those who live in the dark and fearful places
    in the world;
for those crushed with violence because of their faith;
for those facing pain and the evil intentions of others;
for those who are living and worshipping as if Christ is
    not risen but still in the tomb;
for those who have never experienced the joy and the
    freedom and the power
that raised Christ from the dead
and for whom faith means hanging on
    by the skin of their teeth.
May the risen Christ open their hearts.
We ask our prayer,
in the name of Christ.

We pray for those who are afraid of stepping out too far
    into the deep waters of life;
for those who spend their lives in the shallows
and who never experience the wonder of life made new in
    the living Christ;
for those still seeking answers to the meaning of life,
    solutions to their problems,
and an assurance of God's real presence
but who will not risk looking for them
    in the empty tomb.
May the risen Christ transform their hearts.

We ask our prayer,
in the name of Christ.

We pray for our world and for those filled with hatred
   and despair;
for those who never smile, never laugh, never cry;
for those who simply exist when God intended them to live;
for those who settle for instant pleasure
rather than risk opening their lives to the power of Christ;
for those whose lives are ruined as they
   clothe their existence
with addictions that promise everything
   now for a moment;
for those who never hear of God's
   offer of life in abundance
and his promise of heaven because we do not tell them.
May the risen Christ open blind eyes and open sealed lips.
We ask our prayer,
in the name of Christ.

We pray for ourselves.
Lord, give us a new joy in your presence and a new
   awareness that you are alive.
Give us the courage to name your name with our lives
   and our lips.
So fill us, we pray, with your joy and your power,
with your love and your grace, with a trust in your dying
   and an experience of your rising,
that our lives will simply overflow for your glory.
May we have the joy of leading someone to the foot of the
   empty cross to find their Saviour
and to the empty tomb to discover their Lord.
We ask our prayer,
in the name of Christ. Amen.

GIVE THEM HOPE

We pray for those who set out into life with high hopes;
for those who have studied hard and worked with
     determination;
and for those who have shown real commitment and
     faithfulness to the task given to them;
for those who are now filled with deep despair
and a sense of disillusionment as their hopes are dashed
and their dreams have come to nothing
in the harsh reality of life in a fallen world.
May the living Christ give them new hope.
Lord, in your mercy,
hear our prayer.

We pray for those who are overwhelmed by grief
and for those who are filled with regret for what they did
     or failed to do;
for those afraid to think about tomorrow
and for those who, today, still carry a burden of guilt;
for those who cannot let go of the past
and so never enter the new life that is for them;
for those for whom the struggle of living
     each day takes its toll
and for those who long to be free.
May the living Christ give them courage.
Lord, in your mercy,
hear our prayer.

We pray for those who always feel alone or lonely
and for those who are isolated even
     in the midst of a crowd;
for those who are excluded by their colour, their ability,
     their gender, or their singleness;
for those who are locked up in their sense of failure

and for those whose lack of confidence
    is a barrier to progress
and a wall blocking friendships and the discovery of their
    purpose in life.
May the living Christ hold them in his grace.
Lord, in your mercy,
hear our prayer.

We pray for those whose lives are dependent on others
and for those who fight to care for themselves;
for those in the twilight years of their journey
who are dreading the thought of losing their home;
for those who are needing greater support
    than they ever imagined
and for those who provide the care that they need;
for those who take advantage of the goodwill of others
and for those who reject every offer of help.
May the living Christ give them openness to his care.
Lord, in your mercy,
hear our prayer.

We pray for any that we know to be in need of Christ's
    living presence:
for those who are ill or in hospital;
for those who are afraid or alone;
for those who are dying and those who care for them;
for those facing rejection, brokenness, and
    disappointment;
for those whose faith is living and growing;
and for those finding the path of faith hard in our science-
    orientated society.
May the living Christ hold them still.
Lord, in your mercy,
hear our prayer.

We pray for ourselves.
Let us bring our hurts and our hopes, our fears
    and our concerns,
our defeats and our victories to God.
Let us bring our family and friends,
our fellow church members, and ourselves
    to the foot of the cross.
We pray for all we must face in the coming days
    of this week
and our need of God's faithful presence and his life-
    transforming grace.
May the living Christ give us his blessing.
Lord, in your mercy,
hear our prayer.

In the name of Christ, whose presence changes
    everything. **Amen.**

THE JOURNEY

We pray for those whose journey through life
    is filled with pain;
for those who are ill and whose illness
    dominates the whole of their thinking
    and every part of their lives;
for those who may never recover
    and those who care for them;
and those who work or serve in a hospice, a home for the
    elderly, or a nursing home.
May Christ join them on their journey and may they find
    new hope in him.
The Lord hears our prayer.
Thanks be to God.

We pray for those who have lost their way and whose
    journey has become confused
and for those who have lost sight of God and whose faith
    is growing cold;
for those who set out with great enthusiasm and
    anticipation and were committed to Christ
but have now wandered far from the pathway and have
    lost sight of the presence of God.
We pray for those for whom worship, fellowship, prayer,
and Christian service meant everything
but who have now allowed worldly ambitions
    to take their place.
May the living Christ draw near again and warm their
    hearts and lead them home.
The Lord hears our prayer.
Thanks be to God.

We pray for those who are facing a time of great pressure
    and conflict;
for those whose work is frustrating instead of satisfying
    and fulfilling as it once was;
for those whose home life is filled with arguments,
    misunderstanding, and division;
for those who were once committed to those they
    promised to love
and who have now left others feeling empty and lost;
and for those seeking peace, forgiveness,
    and reconciliation.
May the living Christ walk with them and restore them
    in his grace.
The Lord hears our prayer.
Thanks be to God.

We pray for those whose whole life is full
	of negative attitudes
and who always feel that nothing will work for them;
for those who feel they are not worthy
but assume they are unwanted or whose service
	is of little or no value;
for those whose life is crippled by their
	sense of inadequacy
and those whose deep sense of insecurity
prevents them from enjoying the journey at all;
for those who see no end to their anguish
	or their sense of failure
and for whom there is no peace, hope, and love.
May the living Christ walk with them and open their
	hearts and their lives.
The Lord hears our prayer.
Thanks be to God.

We pray for those whose whole life is in a mess;
for those who set out with high hopes
and a genuine determination to honour God in
	everything;
for those for whom each step they now take
is leading them further and further from Christ;
for those who have placed all their hopes on finding
	happiness,
contentment, and a sense of meaning for their lives
through their commitment to gaining wealth
	and material possessions
and who are now finding the emptiness they bring.
May the living Christ set their hearts on fire with the joy
	of his love and presence.
The Lord hears our prayer.
Thanks be to God.

We pray for ourselves and for where we are
    on the journey of life
and for the part we are allowing Christ to play in the
    direction it is taking;
for those moments when we have been especially aware
of him walking with us and those times when we have
    wandered away;
for our concerns and our hopes for ourselves and those for
    whom we care;
for all we are facing on our journey of faith at this moment
and of our need to be ever more open to the work of the
    Spirit within.
May the living Christ make his purposes for our life
    known and his presence a reality.
The Lord hears our prayer.
Thanks be to God.

In the name of Christ. **Amen.**

THE WORD OF CHRIST

Father, we pray for those who are hungry;
for those who are hungry for bread;
for those who are starving for food.
We pray for those in refugee camps with no control
    and no power;
for those who are hungry because of where they live,
the conditions they face mean they are unable to grow
    their own food.
We pray for those who are hungry because of drought,
human foolishness, or human greed.
May the truth of Christ change the world.
Lord, in your mercy,
hear our prayer.

Father, we pray for those who are hungry
      for material possessions;
for those who have so many things but nothing
      that really matters;
for those who put all their energies into the accumulation
      of wealth
and seeking financial security but whose lives are empty
      and whose hearts are cold;
for those who mistakenly think that gaining knowledge,
      experience, and qualifications
will automatically bring their rewards of contentment
      and wisdom.
May the word of Christ teach them his truth.
Lord, in your mercy,
hear our prayer.

Father, we pray for those who are hungry
      for endless activity;
for those who never stand still so that they never see
      themselves as they really are;
for those who are too busy to sit, too busy to think.
We pray for those who are too busy serving God
      and their neighbours
that they have no time just to be still, no time just to be;
for those who are too busy to listen to God
      or to read his Word,
are too busy to pray, which means they are too busy.
May the stillness of Christ feed their restless lives.
Lord, in your mercy,
hear our prayer.

Father, we pray for those who are hungry for life;
for those who know only how to take and need to learn
      how to give;

for those who love to receive but have not learned to share;
for our own nation which has received many riches, yet
    we think we are poor.
We have all we need for life but we think we need more.
We have more than enough but we still lack joy, hope,
    love, and peace.
We have received everything from God's gracious hand
but we have no thankfulness, no sense of
    our dependence on him
to make us more loving to those who have so little.
May the selflessness of Christ conquer our hard hearts
    that all may be fed.
Lord, in your mercy,
hear our prayer.

Father, we pray for those who are hungry for peace;
for those whose hearts and minds are in turmoil;
for those whose lives are disrupted by war or hatred, by
    bitterness or by shame,
by guilt or by failure, by want or despair;
for those who have no sense of their own worth,
those whose lives have been damaged by others'
    selfishness and power;
for those who are hungry to know the peace of God,
to experience his presence and joy.
May the peace of Christ give them hope.
Lord, in your mercy,
hear our prayer.

Father, we pray for those who are hungry for love;
for those who have never known what it means to be
    wanted, needed, and appreciated;
for those who, like all of us, have needed to know that
    they are loved

not for what they do or what they achieve
but to be loved just for themselves and because they are;
for those who from their earliest days have been taught
that love is something they had to earn or be worthy of;
for those who are hungry for unconditional love
    and acceptance.
May the grace of Christ, the free love of God
enable them to accept that they are accepted
    as they are right now.
Lord, in your mercy,
hear our prayer.

In the name of Christ, the true bread of life. **Amen.**

THINK OF SOMEONE

Think of someone who lives alone,
someone who often has no one to talk to for days,
someone who has no one with whom to share
their hopes and fears, their worries and their concerns,
their smiles and their tears.
Ask the Good Shepherd to open their lives to his grace
and your heart to reach out to them with love.

Think of someone who is filled with a sense of
    hopelessness,
someone who is homeless and hungry and for whom the
    future looks bleak.
Think of a refugee with nowhere to call home
and those with homes that have become battlegrounds for
    conflict and hate.
Ask that the arms of the Good Shepherd
and your loving concern may give them hope.

Think of someone in a position of leadership in the world,
someone under great pressure, whose choices and
    decisions
will affect the lives of millions today and the lives of
    generations to come.
Think of someone whose selfish clinging to power
has caused great hurt to their people,
and for someone with a genuine concern for others
and a desire for freedom and power for all.

Think of someone who shows great concern for others,
who risks life and limb for the sake of their neighbour.
Think of those who serve in the police
or the fire, ambulance, or other rescue services.
Think of those who serve God overseas
    as doctors and nurses,
as engineers and teachers, as pastors and farmers.
Think of someone who cares for the homeless, the addicts,
    and the mentally ill.
Ask that the strength of the Good Shepherd
    will be with them.

Think of someone who has been there for you,
someone who has helped you, cared for you,
    and supported you.
Think of someone who has given you courage and hope
and may not know that they have helped you.
Think of someone who made you feel valued, accepted,
    and understood,
someone who by their words and deeds
and by just being there when you need them has shown
    just how much you matter.
Ask that they may know the Good Shepherd's blessing.

Think of yourself and all that is troubling life for you
    right now.
Think of your hopes and your fears, your joys
    and your sorrows,
your successes and failures, your weaknesses and strengths.
Think of your life and how it has been.
Think of your walk with Christ and how he is touching
    and changing you.
Think of how you might allow him to use you to love
    someone else in his name.
Ask the Good Shepherd to walk with you
    and empower you to serve.

Lord, in your mercy,
hear our prayer.

We ask all our prayers in the name of Christ, the Good
    Shepherd. **Amen.**

PRAYERS OF COMMITMENT

LIVING FOR CHRIST

In the midst of a world of pain, we will live for Christ.
For the sake of our neighbours' hurts,
    we will live for Christ.
With those who are lost, empty, sad, or breaking,
    we will live for Christ.
At all times and with all people, we will live for Christ
because Christ is risen and he lives in us. **Amen.**

WE WILL LISTEN

Lord, we commit ourselves to listen for your voice,
to trust your word,
to speak your name,
to live for your glory, and to honour you
in all we say and do and are; for Christ's sake. **Amen.**

NEW HOPE

Father, you have loved us and saved us.
You have held us and healed us and made our lives whole.
You have given us new hope and new life.

You have filled us with your Spirit and fed us
    with your Word.
You have called us in Christ now;
send us in your name to serve you and glorify you for
    ever. **Amen.**

SEEKING YOU

Lord, we commit ourselves to seek you wherever we are
    on the journey
and to be open to your life-transforming power every step
    of the way. **Amen.**

YOU HAVE CALLED US

Lord,
you have called us to take your word of life
    to those who are hurting;
you have filled us with the love of Christ
    to care for the broken;
you have commissioned us to bring hope to the lost
    and the defeated;
you have appointed us to walk with those
    who have no purpose;
you have blessed us and chosen us to love and to care.
Lord, we go in the name of Christ, the true Shepherd of
    all. **Amen.**

PRAYERS OF DISMISSAL

GO

Go with your voice and tell everyone
    that Christ has risen.
Go with your life and show Christ is alive.
Go with your heart and let your love prove it. **Amen.**

TIMES

In times of busyness, find rest in his presence.
In times of quietness, rest in him.
In times of aloneness, feel his arms around you.
In moments of joy and gladness, give him
    thanks and praise.
At all times and in all places, know that he is with you,
    always. **Amen.**

NOURISH US

Lord, nourish us with your grace and fill us
    with your Spirit
that we may receive the promise

and know the joy of eternal life and bring you glory
    throughout our days on earth
and in heaven above. **Amen.**

THE JOURNEY

Lord, the journey is hard and we do not know
    the turnings.
The path is difficult and we can easily lose our way.
The way you have prepared for us is narrow
    and often tests us.
Give us your peace, courage, guidance, and an assurance
    of your living presence
to the end, and beyond. **Amen.**

WITH YOU FOREVER

Jesus says, 'I am the Good Shepherd, you are my sheep.
I know you by name and I will be with you for ever,
    and you with me.' **Amen.**

ABOUT THE AUTHOR

David Clowes, born in Ellesmere Port, left school at fifteen following a secondary modern education. In 1965 he committed his life to Christ at Heaton Mersey Methodist and in 1967 he received God's call into the Methodist ministry. He trained at Hartley Victoria College and gained a degree in theology at the University of Manchester.

David served in a number of churches in the northwest of England before retiring in 2010 after thirty-five years in active ministry. His first book, *500 Prayers for All Occasions*, began as a spiritual exercise during a sabbatical. This was followed by *500 More Prayers for All Occasions*. His third book of prayers, *500 Prayers for the Christian Year*, is based on scriptures from the Revised Common Lectionary.

David is married to Angela, and they have two married sons, a foster son, and four grandchildren.